Identity

Created Woman Devotional Series

2022

Volume 5, Issue 3

Stacy Barbeau / Heather Bise / Crystal Breaux
Martha Bush / Heather Frierson / Mae Grant
Treasure Johnson / Stacy McVane / Alex Parsons

Copyright © 2022 Created Woman
ISBN: 9798834796527

All rights reserved.

No part of this publication may be reproduced, stored in a retrieval system, or transmitted in any way by any means—electronic, mechanical, photocopy, recording or otherwise—without the prior permission of the author except as provided by the USA Copyright Law.

This book is designed to provide accurate and authoritative information with regard to the subject matter covered. This information is given with the understanding that neither the author nor the publisher is engaged in rendering legal, professional advice. Since the details of your situation are fact dependent, you should additionally seek the services of a competent professional as needed.

Scripture quotations marked MSG from The Message. Copyright © by Eugene H. Peterson 1993, 1994, 1995, 1996, 2000, 2001, 2002. Used by permission of Tyndale House Publishers, Inc.

Scripture quotations marked NASB® taken from the New American Standard Bible®, Copyright © 1960, 1962, 1963, 1968, 1971, 1972, 1973, 1975, 1977, 1995 by The Lockman Foundation. Used by permission. All rights reserved. www.lockman.org

Scripture quotations marked NIV are taken from the Holy Bible, New International Version®, NIV®. Copyright © 1973, 1978, 1984, 2011 by Biblica, Inc.™ Used by permission of Zondervan. All rights reserved worldwide. www.zondervan.com The "NIV" and "New International Version" are trademarks registered in the United States Patent and Trademark Office by Biblica, Inc.™

Scripture marked NKJV taken from the New King James Version®. Copyright © 1982 by Thomas Nelson. Used by permission. All rights reserved.

Scripture quotations marked NLT are taken from the Holy Bible, New Living Translation, copyright ©1996, 2004, 2007, 2013 by Tyndale House Foundation. Used by permission of Tyndale House Publishers, Inc., Carol Stream, Illinois 60188. All rights reserved.

Scripture quotations marked TPT are from The Passion Translation®. Copyright © 2017, 2018 by Passion & Fire Ministries, Inc. Used by permission. All rights reserved. ThePassionTranslation.com.

Dedicated to the community of women who are learning to dream, live life on purpose, and explore their faith.

CONTENTS

	Acknowledgments	1
	Created Woman: Principles, Vision, Mission	2
	Letter from Our Founder	3
	About This Devotional	5
1	Top Five (Stacy McVane)	9
2	No Regrets (Heather Bise)	13
3	A Counselor Says . . . (Mae Grant)	17
4	Where Do the God Girls Go to Hide Away? (Alex Parsons)	21
5	My Go-To Fruit (Crystal Breaux)	25
6	Don't Trade Rubies for Rocks! (Stacy Barbeau)	29
7	Identity Transformation (Martha Bush)	33
8	Great Minds Thinks Alike (Treasure Johnson)	37
	Dream Launcher (EMPOWER)ment Session	41
	Meet the CW Family Writers	43

ACKNOWLEDGMENTS

To the women we have the honor of serving:
We love you and are cheering and praying for you daily. Because you continue to go after your dreams and purpose, you inspire us to do the same.

To our Created Woman family:
Thank you for saying yes to equipping and empowering HER to be all SHE is created to be.
You are all Legacy Builders!

CreatedWoman.Net

@createdwoman

CREATED WOMAN

Community of women learning to dream,
live life on purpose, and explore our faith
through gatherings, resources, podcast, and mentorship.

PRINCIPLES
DREAMS • HEALING • IDENTITY
PURPOSE • HEALTH • FASHION

VISION
Created woman exists to equip and empower women to be who they are created to be inside & out.

MISSION
Created Woman's mission is to turn dreams into purpose and women into leaders through mentorship, coaching, gatherings, resources, and community because we believe that as you change a woman's life, she changes the world around her.

Through six core principles we empower women to dream, run with endurance, show up well as an Ambassador of Christ, and live a life unleashed, reacting to the purpose God has given them and forever changing the world for generations to come.

TURNING DREAMS INTO PURPOSE, WOMEN INTO LEADERS

Letter from Our Founder

Identity: What's So Confusing?

No matter where I look, it seems to have become the norm for people to choose an identity that doesn't necessarily line up with who God actually created them to be.

The question of Identity, or who we are, first shows up in the heart asking, "Who are you, really?" It's a question we all must face not just one time in our lives, but if we reflect for a moment, I'm sure we can all remember several times when we had to sit and ask, "Who am I?"

It can happen after all the big moments in life: high school or college graduation, marriage, divorce, having a baby, losing a job or a loved one. There's a kind of void that creeps in that makes us question, "Where do I fit?"

Created Woman asks you the question all the time, "Who were you created to be?" Do you know? Have you cleared out the clutter, the noise of the world, to really find out what God has for you, who He uniquely created you to be? Or have you allowed yourself to be tossed to and fro, not stopping to consider your answers to these questions?

Think on this: do you view your identity from a biblical perspective, or have cultural beliefs influenced your thinking in this area?

The truth is, God made us who we are so we could make known who He is. Our identity is for the sake of making known his identity.

So today I challenge you to settle the noise around you and really start having the tough conversations with yourself, with God, and with your children. Ask the questions you fear to ask. Talk about the things that make you uncomfortable. Stretch yourself to open the love letter that was written for you (the Bible) and begin to study it. I promise, you'll start to hear what God has just for you and for your children, allowing you to discover an identity that's rooted in Christ and is never tossed to and fro.

XOXO,

Heather

ABOUT THIS DEVOTIONAL

HOW TO READ – WHAT YOU NEED

How to Read:

The Created Woman Devotional Series is designed for both interactive study with your Dream Launcher friend or for group discussion. Here are a few suggestions for making your time with the study more meaningful.

First, this devotional is written in a way to be interactive so that you can truly experience a transformation in your own life. In order to do that, considering each reflection question and answering thoughtfully at the end of each day is the best way to digest what you just read.

The section called "Goal Setting" is where you will write down 3 goals based on the daily devotional. Take as much time as you want in these sections. There may be some things you have to work through in order to get to the next step in your life. If so, forget about the structure and reflect on just one day for as long as you need.

Reflect + Pray + Listen = Transformation!

Second, at the end of the devotional, make an appointment with your Dream Launcher friend. Together, you will:
- Fill out the Dream Launcher (Empower)ment Session at the end of the devotional.
- Discuss the questions on conversation cards.

What You Need:
1. This devotional
2. Bible
3. Journal
4. Time set aside each day and once a month or week with your group or Dream Launcher friend.

Dream Launcher Friend:

We truly believe that we should not do this thing called "life" alone. In fact, Jesus tells us in Genesis 2:18 that it is not good for man to be alone. When we do things with a trusted friend who is also a believer, God-sized dreams become more attainable as we pray together. So choose wisely. Choose a girlfriend who is trustworthy and reliable, who keeps things in confidence, who believes in the Bible, and who is faithful to meet with you every week.

By connecting with our Dream Launcher friends, the ones we celebrate and cry with, we are able to take one dream step at a time and soar to new heights. Simply, spending time with our friends and just being able to be ourselves is what makes life a little fuller and more enjoyable!

What now?

Usually with each new season, whether it's a graduation, baby, marriage, new job, or move, our purpose tends to look and feel a little different. We find ourselves asking, "What now?" That's why we do the 6 principles twice a year so that you don't lose focus! As you begin your journey, just be encouraged with this:

Your purpose will never change, but your strategy will constantly change.

Okay, are you ready to become the woman you were created to be? You have a whole tribe cheering and praying for you! We believe in you, and we believe that God has created you on purpose and for a purpose. So let's do this!

XOXO,

Heather Frierson

> *Then the L*ORD *replied:*
> *"Write down the revelation*
> *and make it plain on tablets*
> *so that a herald may run with it.*
> *For the revelation awaits an appointed time;*
> *it speaks of the end*
> *and will not prove false.*
> *Though it linger, wait for it;*
> *it will certainly come*
> *and will not delay."*
> *(Habakkuk 2:2–3 NIV)*

> *It's better to have a partner than go it alone. Share the work, share the wealth. And if one falls down, the other helps, but if there's no one to help, tough! Two in a bed warm each other. Alone, you shiver all night. By yourself you're unprotected. With a friend you can face the worst. Can you round up a third? A three-stranded rope isn't easily snapped.*
> *(Ecclesiastes 4:9–12 MSG)*

TOP FIVE
Setting Priorities Geared to Your Identity in Christ

By Stacy McVane

When I am with those who are weak, I share their weakness, for I want to bring the weak to Christ. Yes, I try to find common ground with everyone, doing everything I can to save some. I do everything to spread the Good News and share in its blessings.
(1 Corinthians 9:22–23 NLT)

For we are His workmanship, created in Christ Jesus for good works, which God prepared beforehand that we should walk in them.
(Ephesians 2:10 NKJV)

I have a top five:
1. Faith (Jesus, community with others who have shared values, church involvement)
2. Relationships (family, friends, man in my life—soon, Jesus, soon, please!)
3. Career
4. Exercise (Orangetheory and stretching) and nutrition
5. Created Woman

What does having a top five mean? It means the top five things I focus on in my life. Why? It is easy to get distracted and pulled in different directions. I have been distracted a time or two (or two hundred). When I am distracted, I get drained, frustrated, and burned out. I get edgy: easily irritated and short in conversations. I have even caught myself picking fights with people in my head. That's when I notice I'm not looking for opportunities to make a difference in the lives of others. I'm not asking questions out of curiosity or taking the time to listen. I'm not encouraging and fun. I'm not surrendered to God and asking for help. I'm filling my calendar and saying yes without consulting the Holy Spirit. My calendar is full and my relationship with God gets put on the back burner.

In 1 Corinthians 9:22–23, the apostle Paul is encouraging us to find common ground with others and do everything to spread the good news. I notice that Paul doesn't say, "Go to every gathering you are invited to, serve everywhere and every time you get asked, and don't take care of yourself or your home." In order to have enough energy for my life, what God has called me to do, I stick to my top five. I also do my laundry, sleep, pack my lunch, and have someone clean my home once a month.

Now, don't get me wrong, I still have fun. After all, my motto is, "If it's not fun, I'm not doing it." My top five is part of my identity, the way God created me: efficient, organized, and intentional. Ephesians 2:10 says that I'm created to do great things that God already has planned for me. He created me to be structured, organized, decisive, and efficient. When I am flowing in my top five, it's an absolute blast. I'm focused and see the opportunities in front of me to encourage people, pray for people, and be present. But the best part is that I am making a difference in the lives of others. When I do that, I'm energized and fulfilled, and I'm glorifying God. That makes an impact for the cause of Christ by developing disciples.

Reflection

1. What or who energizes you?
   _____
   _____
   _____

2. What or who makes you drained or frustrated?
   _____
   _____
   _____

3. List three to five character traits that you know are part of your identity in Christ. Now that's a reason to be proud of the way God made you.
   _____
   _____
   _____

Goal Setting

Write one goal you can accomplish this week (at home, at work, with family, etc.) that will help you focus on your God-given identity:
_____
_____
_____

NO REGRETS

Does Christianity Guarantee a Regret-Free Life?

By Heather Bise

> *But you are a chosen people, a royal priesthood, a holy nation, God's special possession, that you may declare the praises of him who called you out of darkness into his wonderful light.*
> (1 Peter 2:9 NIV)

As I enter middle age, I have some pretty big regrets. Looking back at missteps and missed opportunities, I struggle not to go down the rabbit hole of judgment. There are the average regrets where I think about times I should have spoken up, shut my mouth, or worked harder at something.

Then there is The One Huge Regret: I wish I had done things better for my son before he died.

That is the one that threatens my identity the most. Who am I if I was not a better mother when I had the opportunity? Do I even consider myself a "good" Christian? Can God bless me again after fumbling the greatest blessing I had?

Some regrets are simply insurmountable. There are some things that cannot be changed, but let me tell you, in Christ all things can be redeemed.

Like all emotions, regret cannot be avoided. We can try, but to say you will live a life of no regrets is like saying you will live a life where you never find anything funny as long as you live. Pain, anger, frustration, grief, and regret are guaranteed to be a part of the human experience. They do not mean God is displeased with you, punishing you, testing you, or lifting His hand of blessing from you. They are just emotions, and Scripture gives us plenty of resources to handle them in a responsible and godly way.

No matter how I feel, God has never removed the gift of salvation and eternal life from me. I will never be exempt from what the work of the cross accomplished. Fruitfulness and contentment are always available to me as a child of God, by way of the Holy Spirit working in me and the Word of God empowering me to take hold of the kingdom of heaven while still here on Earth.

My value is never compromised by my actions or inaction. My joy is overflowing that I am one in the Spirit with God, and so is my son. In that way, my son and I are very much connected, and as he now is in the great cloud of witnesses, he can know my heart and intentions in a way that renders regret powerless. That, my friends, is a miraculous redemption for my shortsighted foolishness—a lavish gift I can never repay but one God finds me worthy to receive because I am His daughter.

When I contemplate all God has done through the cross, I am overwhelmed by the thought that there is nothing God cannot redeem, restore, or reclaim on my behalf. It is also amazing that there is no feeling I can feel that removes me from His grace. His grace is boundless, and to think I could do something big enough to negate it is ridiculous.

Putting regret in perspective under the shadow of the great work of the cross sweeps me away on the tide of another emotion: gratitude. There is no place where I do not have intrinsic value to God. I am beloved because I am His, and nothing can change that.

Reflection

1. What are some regrets you have?

   _____
   _____
   _____

2. How do these regrets make you feel?

   _____
   _____
   _____

3. Name some things Scripture says about Christ's redemption. Do you believe these things apply to you?

   _____
   _____
   _____

Goal Setting

Look up three things the Bible says that the cross accomplished and write them below. How do these truths speak to your regrets?

1. _____
2. _____
3. _____

A Counselor Says . . .

Remembering What the Ultimate Counselor Says About Our Identity

By Mae Grant

For unto us a Child is born, unto us a Son is given; and the government will be upon His shoulder. And His name will be called Wonderful, Counselor, Mighty God, Everlasting Father, Prince of Peace.
(Isaiah 9:6 NKJV)

Where there is no counsel, the people fall; but in the multitude of counselors there is safety.
(Proverbs 11:14 NKJV)

Hey girl, yours truly here—a nationally certified counselor, a licensed professional counselor associate, and a school counselor—and it turns out I do *not* know everything I thought I would by now. What?! I know, several years of graduate school studying all the mental health disorders possible for the human psyche, and you heard it here first: I still have a lot to learn and that's okay.

I titled this devotional "A Counselor Says . . ." for a reason. I don't know about you, but I'm always looking to improve, so I definitely want to know what a counselor is saying. They *must* know all the answers regarding how to help anyone and everyone, right? Here's a secret for you: we don't. We are constantly learning along with all of our clients. However, our superpower is that we *do* know how to form relationships. That being said, I'll tell you a little about my experience and why I believe counseling and our identity in Christ are linked.

When I was in grad school, my favorite and probably the most important thing I learned about counseling was how to develop relationships with clients. I learned that there are three things necessary for a good relationship with a client:
1. Unconditional positive regard
2. Empathy
3. Reflection of feeling and content

For example, if a client comes into counseling and states that they are having a hard time with self-worth, we express genuinely how difficult it must be to struggle with that and reflect back their self-worth journey while being with them emotionally in every moment. Easier said than done.

It's not all about the content or the solutions being shared; it's even more about the comfort the client feels and the relationship they have with their counselor. If anything about the client-counselor relationship is off, you can forget about getting anywhere. I went through five different counselors before I found mine (yes, it's an unspoken requirement for a counselor to have their own counselor), so I know how it feels when you hit that magic spot of finding one you trust completely. I have a faith-based counselor, and we talk often about my where my worth and identity come from, which is what the ultimate Counselor has to say. Who's the ultimate Counselor, you ask? God.

I think it is human to look everywhere for answers that help us define who we are. We ask questions, such as, "How can I heal, grow, and be who I want to be?" I know I've sat in the chair as a client and wanted my counselor to help me explore all of these areas. What I have found in therapy is that anyone in a helping profession has tremendous value and definitely a place in this world. However, without a foundation of Christ it's impossible to go on the journey. It's through our relationship with God as a loving, gracious Father that we can even go on the journey at all. We can go talk to a counselor all day long about what has been plaguing us, but if it's not pointing us back to Jesus, we should probably rethink our approach. The ultimate Counselor is God, and there's no more important relationship than the one you have with Him. Any time I am questioning my identity and where my worth comes from, I remember it comes from the ultimate Counselor. Having a relationship with Him and remembering his Word is key, knowing that earthly counseling is here only to guide us not to give us that worth, but the ultimate Counselor gives us truth.

Reflection

1. How does God, the ultimate Counselor, give you guidance in your life?

   _____
   _____
   _____

2. How can you define your identity according to God's Word?

   _____
   _____

3. What scriptures can you meditate on to help you remember that your identity and self-worth come from Him?

   _____
   _____
   _____

Goal Setting

Write one goal you can accomplish this week (at home, at work, with family, etc.) that will apply to your life what God is revealing to you in this devotional:

_____
_____
_____

Where Do the God Girls Go to Hide Away?

Created to Be Seen and Known

By Alex Parsons

*The Lord God made garments of skin for Adam
and his wife and clothed them.*
(Genesis 3:21 NIV)

*Faith has immersed you into Christ, and now you
are covered and clothed with His life.*
(Galatians 3:27 TPT)

Allowing myself to be seen and known in relationships has been one of my life's biggest struggles. In every type of relationship I've had, it's been hard for me to be completely honest and open. The kind of visceral anxiety I would experience in my body when I tried to dive into the deep knowingness with another is what put me in the office of my new counselor.

To be honest, my hiding was so bad that I would rarely ever even tell someone I didn't like something that was offered to me; I'd just grin and bear whatever it was. I kept so much of my thoughts and heart to myself. I didn't even feel safe enough to tell someone not to put beans on my plate. I hate beans! Why was this so hard?

I sought out a counselor to help me with this burden, and one day she asked me, "What was the first memory you have of your life and childhood?" I sat for a moment thinking about what I remembered about some of my earliest experiences in childhood.

The memories cascaded into my mind like a flood.

I suddenly remembered so vividly.

I can remember being around four or five years old, hiding away in a hallway closet among sleeping bags and extra blankets. I remember how comfortable and slightly mischievous it felt to be so snuggled up and mysteriously tucked away with no one knowing where I was. As a child I recall this being a place of peace, and who knows how long I would hide away in that closet left unseen and unsought.

I think it's interesting and worth noting that in the Bible, after sin enters into God's perfectly created world, the first thing humans want to do is hide (Gen. 3:8). They hide their bodies, and they hide from God, and God clothed—i.e., covered—them. This really stood out to me in my morning reading time several years ago. Since then my experiences, not only in my relationship with the Lord but in all my close relationships, have taught me that the solution to the urge to hide is to allow God to cover us in our vulnerability. We don't need to hide if we're *covered*.

Another early memory I have as a child is being held by my father after he returned from being in the military overseas. I remember searching the crowds for him and knowing I would recognize him as soon as I saw his face. As he held me in his arms, I felt pure joy. His presence and scruffy face made me feel so incredibly safe and at peace. This moment is one of my favorite memories. Through this image, the Lord has revealed to me that as long as I am in His presence with my heart safely nuzzled next to Him, I am safe in any space or relationship.

I am free to be myself whether someone chooses to embrace me or not, because I'm already covered and embraced by Christ. It is in this freedom that I'm able to let my loved ones truly know me. It's in this security I can safely say, "Hey, actually, I would prefer not to have a side of beans, please."

Reflection

1. Do you feel seen and known by God?
   _____
   _____
   _____

2. Do you feel like you can be open and honest with God about your heart? Why or why not?
   _____
   _____
   _____

3. What is a verse in the Bible that makes you feel safe and covered by God?
   _____
   _____
   _____

Goal Setting

Schedule time with one person this week with whom you feel you can be yourself, and spend some time intentionally connecting with them about their life too. Describe your experience below:
_____
_____
_____

MY GO-TO FRUIT
The Many Lasting Benefits of Closeness with the Spirit

By Crystal Breaux

"But the fruit of the Spirit is love, joy, peace, forbearance, kindness, goodness, faithfulness, gentleness and self-control.
(Galatians 5:22 NIV)

"I am an anxious person."
"I have anger issues."
"I can't help myself."
"I am just weak."
"This will always be my struggle."

Are these words and labels, which many women often use to define themselves, familiar to you? Do you sometimes wonder if you will always be "that person"?

If we accept these definitions of ourselves, we will continue to walk in a state of anxiousness, bitterness, resentment, or weakness, imprisoned by that one thing we identity ourselves to be. Our attitude can keep us from walking in the freedom of God and everything He wants us to be.

I have a natural impulse to get things done. However, in my effort to get something done, I can spout off unnecessary words or carry out actions that cause damage, hurt, or mistakes. In those times, I have to take a deep breath and be reminded of Galatians 5:22 (NLT), which clearly defines the fruit of the Spirit as "love, joy, peace, patience, kindness, goodness, faithfulness, gentleness, and self-control." These are the characteristics we are to identify with as followers of Christ. I have to say that in my natural state, when I want to get things done, self-control would definitely not always be a ripened fruit in my life. I can be so consumed with what I need and want to *do*, I forget what I need to *be*. The truth is that those negative definitions we have given ourselves can hold us back from doing what the Lord would have us do and from living as a reflection of Christ Jesus.

The good news is that we do not have to accept that we are destined always to be "that person." First Peter 1 says that we are children of God and He has given us power and authority. The things I cannot demonstrate self-control for on my own, I can tap into the help and authority I have as a child of God. I no longer have to claim, "That's just how I am."

My friends, we no longer have to be mastered by our thoughts, fears, desires, worries, laziness, doubts, self-talk, addictions, or anger, or any other stronghold (you fill in the blank). We can turn our hearts toward God and give our struggles to Him. As we connect to Him each day, He can begin to mold us into women who are identified with the fruit of the Spirit.

Reflection

1. As you reflect on the fruit of the Spirit, which one do you identity with least in your natural state?
   _____
   _____
   _____

2. If you were to develop that fruit, what is an example of how it would be revealed in your life each day?

   _____
   _____
   _____

3. What can you do to connect with the Lord each day to grow in Him and in developing the fruit of the Spirit (e.g., spend time in His Word, memorize the fruit of the Spirit, talk with someone in your life who exemplifies the fruit of the Spirit)?

   _____
   _____
   _____

Goal Setting

What is one fruit of the Spirit you would like to develop and one action you can take today to move closer in that direction?

_____
_____
_____

Don't Trade Rubies for Rocks!
Understanding Who and Whose We Are

By Stacy Barbeau

*Praise be to God and Father of our Lord Jesus Christ, who has **blessed us** in the heavenly realms with every spiritual blessing in Christ. For he **chose us** in him before the creation of the world to be holy and blameless in his sight. In love he **predestined us** for adoption to sonship through Jesus Christ, in accordance with his pleasure and will—to the praise of his glorious grace, which he has freely given us in the One he loves.*
(Ephesians 1:3–6 NIV, emphasis mine)

When I was nine years old, I accepted Jesus Christ as my Lord and Savior at a church camp. I was young and definitely did not fully comprehend the gravity of Christ's love, or the true meaning of Christianity, but I knew I wanted to be a part of it and to know Jesus more!

Now fast-forward to college, and I still did not fully know my identity in Christ Jesus. Thus, I made some bad decisions! I allowed sin to take over a large part of the time. Then, following college and entering into my professional, "adult" life, I quickly realized that I needed to change my life. I needed to act like the Christian I claimed to be, strive to become like Jesus, and truly live for Him and His glory. After lots of prayer, Jesus redeeming me in His powerful blood, becoming part of a strong church community, and having great friends who push me forward in my journey with Jesus and in my identity in Christ, today I am now at a point where I can confidently say I know my identity in Christ and my value to my Creator.

Identity has become an idol for our generation. People look to sex, race, and work, among other things, to find their identity because they truly don't know who they are; they are searching for significance in something that is less significant. This was exactly me in college. I traded rubies for rocks!

However, in Ephesians 1:3–6 (NIV), Paul writes, "Praise be to the God and Father of our Lord Jesus Christ, who has **blessed us** in the heavenly realms with every spiritual blessing in Christ. For he **chose us** in him before the creation of the world to be holy and blameless in his sight. In love he **predestined us** for adoption to sonship through Jesus Christ, in accordance with his pleasure and will—to the praise of his glorious grace, which he has freely given us in the One he loves." From this passage we learn three things. God **blessed us** abundantly. God also literally handpicked each and every one of us. He knew we would be saved before the world was even created! Lastly, he **predestined us** for adoption to sonship through Jesus Christ. This means we did not choose God but God **chose us**! He did not choose us for anything that we have done or will do! God elected us to serve His purpose for His glory, because he *loves us*! He chose to save us because he *loves us*!

If I could go back and talk to twenty-something-year-old Stacy in college, I would tell her, "Girl, God *chose* you and has a grand plan for your life, all because he *loves* you and *wants* you!" He chose me, Stacy, knowing the sins I would commit, and still made a way to redeem me, that I should be set apart, holy, and blameless in his sight. Let this be encouragement for you today in your identity in Christ! You are blessed, you are chosen, you are predestined, and most importantly, you are saved and greatly loved by the Creator of the world! Do not choose rocks when you are given rubies! You are far too precious!

Reflection

1. Discuss with your Dream Launcher friend a time when you "traded rocks for rubies." What was the situation, and what was going on that you felt the need to "trade rocks for rubies"? Were you feeling insecure, unsure of your identity, or both?

   _____
   _____
   _____

2. Describe a time when you clung to your identity in Christ, realizing your worth and the immense love God has for us. What is the difference in the way you felt, the way you carried yourself, etc. from the situation listed in question 1?

   _____
   _____
   _____

3. What advice would you give to a younger version of yourself, like I imagine speaking to twenty-something-year-old Stacy? What advice can you give to others who are struggling with thinking they need to trade in their rubies for rocks?

   _____
   _____
   _____

Goal Setting

Discuss two to three goals with your Dream Launcher friend regarding how you can renew your mind daily to ensure that your future self does not make the mistake of trading "rubies for rocks," instead standing strong in your identity in Christ Jesus. Write these goals below:

1. _____
2. _____
3. _____

IDENTITY TRANSFORMATION
Transform Your Mind to Know Your Identity

By Martha Bush

And do not be conformed to this world, but be transformed by the renewing of your mind, that you may prove what is that good and acceptable and perfect will of God.
(Romans 12:2 NKJV)

Many of us can relate to this scripture: "Why are you cast down, O my soul? And why are you disquieted within me? Hope in God; for I shall yet praise Him, the help of my countenance and my God" (Ps. 42:11 NKJV).

We often get stuck in this place of feeling cast down and weary because we are dreaming of a day when our circumstances will change. In the story of Leah, Jacob, and Rachel, as found in Genesis 29–30, it was Leah who had every reason to feel cast down and disquieted. Can you imagine being rejected and unloved by your own husband? Can you even fathom living in the same house with your husband and your sister, the woman he loves?

When the Lord saw how Jacob was treating Leah, He opened her womb, but Rachel remained barren. Leah thought that after the birth of child number one, two, and three, her husband would profess his love to her, but he didn't. However, when Leah's fourth son was born, she said, "Now I will praise the Lord" (Gen. 29:35 NKJV).

Obviously, a transformation had taken place in Leah between the third son and the fourth son. What was that transformation? I personally believe that, at last, she realized her identity and worth were in the one true God who loved, accepted, affirmed, and saw her for the beautiful woman she was. She no longer waited for her circumstances to change; instead, she realized who she was in Christ, and her identity was not based on any man's approval or love for her. And with that, her weariness gave birth to praise.

I have been there. Waiting for circumstances and people to change once caused me to be stuck in a perpetual state of weariness, not to mention the fact that I had no idea who I was. Just like Leah, the Lord saw my state of mind, and He began leading me step-by-step to a place of spiritual and emotional healing. A transformation took place in me without my circumstances changing.

Having accepted Jesus Christ as my Savior many years ago, I became a new creation with access to many benefits, such as a new destination of heaven once I passed from this earth, the Holy Spirit coming to live within me to guide me, and a new heart that wanted to please my heavenly Father.

While there was an instantaneous change in my spiritual nature, I was still dealing with my old fleshly nature. In essence, my spirit was renewed, but my mind had to be renewed from old thought patterns in order to be transformed like the Bible says: "And do not be conformed to this world, but be transformed by the renewing of your mind, that you may prove what is that good and acceptable and perfect will of God" (Rom. 12:2 NKJV).

As a result of faithfully availing myself to Bible study, both privately and with others, my mind was renewed. Now I can say that my soul is no longer cast down and disquieted. My hope is in

God, the help of my countenance, and I praise Him for showing me that my identity and worth are in Him, not in my circumstances or people's approval of me.

Reflection

1. What do you feel is the main obstacle, if any, standing in your way of knowing your identity in Christ?

   _____
   _____
   _____

2. How can renewing your mind, as discussed in this devotional, help you get past this obstacle?

   _____
   _____
   _____

3. What steps can you take to renew your mind so that it is transformed from your old nature (e.g., more Bible study, counseling, etc.)?

   _____
   _____
   _____

Goal Setting

Referring back to question #3 and the steps you listed to renew your mind, write one goal to begin with to accomplish those steps:

_____
_____
_____

GREAT MINDS THINK ALIKE
Thinking What God Thinks of You

By Treasure Johnson

As he thinks within himself, so he is.
(Proverbs 23:7 NASB)

    I don't know about you, but I know there have been many days in my life where honestly I was just floating along. Yes, I had a goal, I had a plan, and I even had a big dream, but in most moments, I just felt so stuck. I can remember many days staring at the ceiling, eating my M&M's, and hoping that things could just be easier. The days that I spent in my bed are the days that the devil tried to plant these thoughts about myself that were not true in my head and in my heart. They sounded like "Look at you, you're just being lazy!" and, "Yeah, you are never going to get done." Sadly, I started to believe that what he was saying might be true.

    One thing we know about the devil is that he is a liar. So anything that he might try to say to us, we can automatically believe the opposite. I went back to the Word, as I often do, and in Proverbs 23:7 (NASB), it says, "As he thinks within himself, so he is." Translation? Whatever you think about yourself, that is what you are.

    This is where having a community that can uplift you and remind you to replace those negative thoughts with positive ones is vital. You need a tribe that can remind you about who you are in God's eyes! Knowing God's Word so you can know what He says about you is the best way to stop those thoughts that might try to come in and make you feel bad about yourself.

The powerful thing about God is He gives life with his words. That means everything God says is true, and *it will happen*. He says you are blessed, and so you are! He says you are more than an overcomer, and you are! He says that you have freedom to let go of things that were once hurting you, and you do! If those are things that God has spoken over you, and you know God is stronger than the devil, whose thoughts will you partner yours with? Believe that you are an amazing woman who was created on purpose, for a purpose . . . and you will be.

Reflection

1. When you feel stuck, what is the first thing you tend to do? (Mine is eating M&M's.)

   _____
   _____
   _____

2. Who do you have around you that can support and empower you from a faith-based perspective?

   _____
   _____
   _____

3. Is it easy or difficult for you to put God's thoughts about you first? Why do you think this is?

   _____
   _____
   _____

Goal Setting

Find four scriptures that speak to who God says you are, and pray those truths daily for the rest of the month.

1. _____
2. _____
3. _____
4. _____

SHARE LISTEN EQUIP EMPOWER

Dream Launcher (EMPOWER)ment Session

This section is dedicated to sharing a process of growth and empowerment with a friend who will hold you accountable and support you through your journey.

My Dream Launcher is:
(name)_____

We regularly meet on (list day of week or how often you meet):_____

Dare to share — Share your dreams for 3–5 minutes. Take this time to **dream out loud** and share your goals and hopes.

Reflect — Take time to reflect on what the other person shared and offer feedback. What did you hear them say? Can you pick up on any themes?

Elaborate — Ask more in-depth questions to get more details regarding goals and identify three **DREAM Steps** (see below) that can be taken before next session.

Apply and alternate — Once you have helped identify dream steps, write them down and take turns sharing.

<u>M</u>otivate — Do you have any words of advice or encouragement? Offer contacts or suggestions for next steps.

DREAM Steps:

List the three steps you've identified to take before your next meeting with your Dream Launcher.

1._____
_____
_____
_____

2._____
_____
_____
_____

3._____
_____
_____
_____

Meet the CW Family Writers & Follow:

Stacy Barbeau: : IG @stbarbeau
Heather Bise: IG @heather.bise.7
Crystal Breaux: IG @crystal_g_breaux
Martha Bush: FB @martha.bush.39
Heather Frierson: IG @heatherfrierson29
Mae Grant: IG @maemariegrant
Treasure Johnson: IG @treasure.johnson_
Stacy McVane: IG @stacylmcvane
Alex Parsons: IG @youremyparsons

Additional Thanks To:

Katie Landers (blog editor): IG @katie.landers.3
Marina Marston (cover photographer):
IG @squareearthstudio
Deb Hall (manuscript editor): IG @debhall333

Made in the USA
Columbia, SC
29 June 2022